Other books of BIZARRO cartoons: BIZARRO
TOO BIZARRO
MONDO BIZARRO
SUMO BIZARRO
GLASNOST BIZARRO
POST-MODERN BIZARRO
THE BEST OF BIZARRO
THE BEST OF BIZARRO vol. II

## Attention: SCHOOLS and BUSINESSES

Andrews and McMeel books are available at quantity discounts with bulk purchase for educational, business, or sales promotional use. For information, please write to: Special Sales Department, Andrews and McMeel, 4900 Main Street, Kansas City, Missouri 64112.

To contact Dan Piraro directly, try one of his e-mail addresses: BIZARRO95@AOL.COM or BIZARRO@CIS.COMPUSERVE.COM which may or may not still be valid accounts by the time you see this message, depending on how well this book sells. Or write to him at this "real" world address: Dan Piraro, c/o Andrews and McMeel, 4900 Main Street, Kansas City, Missouri 64112.

This book, like the 8 before it, is dedicated to the fabulous K's; Kalin, my wonderwife, the Incredible Killian and the Amazing Kaitlin. They live in blatant defiance of the stereotype that a woman cannot be both beautiful & brilliant.

Special thanks to my good friend BART ODOM, whose loyal support & critical reader→ ship together with an off-hand remark over dinner inspired me to wake up & smell the camels. He has also proved to be an invaluable collaborator (when properly supervised).

Thanks also to all of the folks who've e-mailed me this year. I've enjoyed our little chats & cherish your support & encouragement. Those listed below are but a few of the most frequent writers. My apologies to those I've left off the list — my recordkeeping sucks...

AJ, Alice, Bill, Boaz, Bob, Chris, Cindy, Dan, Dave, David, Debroder, Don, Doug, Edward, Eric, Erika, Helene, Hisako, Jackie, Jared, Jason, Jeff, Jerry, Jiji, John, Josh, Kami, Karen, Kate, Ken, Lizzy, Maggie, Manu, Mark, Marty, Matt, Neil, Phil, Richard, Rick, Roger, Eggplant, Shane, Steve, Strange, Sue, Tim, Tom, Tongel, Tony, Traci, Zac. And, as always, cheers to the Semi-Official Canadian FanClub & Motor Oil Company.

Library of Congress Catalog Card Number: 95-77569

ISBN: 0-8362-0430-1

(And people think my *cartoons* are wordy.)

# A Few Words From Your Old Pal, Dan...

How many times have you heard people say of the comics page, "man, this stuff blows!" Well, maybe not in those words, but the truth is that most people think that most newspaper comics aren't funny. The problem is, with a few notable exceptions (and we all know which ones those are), people don't agree on *which ones* aren't funny. Sadly, many editors think that features like BIZARRO are too clever or strange for the average reader. You and I know that's not true, but we must make our voices heard.

BIZARRO is a nationally syndicated newspaper comic that appears 7 days a week. If you like these comics and your paper doesn't carry BIZARRO, or doesn't carry it every day, please write or call the comics editor of your local paper and ask them to do so. If your paper already carries BIZARRO, tell them you appreciate it and hope they don't cancel it. All your friendly editor wants is to please you, the reader, but they can't do it if they don't know what you want. Won't you help me help you to help yourself and your community? Please call now. Thank you.

SQEAKY
the Talking
Chihuahua
"I'LL G͠ET IT!"

IT WORKS A LOT LIKE A SEEING-EYE DOG.... HE RINGS THE BELL ONCE FOR "STOP", TWICE FOR "GO", AND IF HE FLIES AWAY COMPLETELY, I KNOW THERE'S A CAT IN THE ROOM.

YES, OFFICERS, HE'S MY HUSBAND — AND I'VE TOLD HIM A THOUSAND TIMES, " CHANGE YOUR CLOTHES *BEFORE* YOU WALK HOME FROM THE BUTCHER SHOP LATE AT NIGHT."

**6**

HOW CAMOUFLAGE WORKS

BRUNO IMPRESSES HIS DATE WITH A FOREIGN LANGUAGE.

INVENTION OF THE TELEPHONE BOOK

Another comedian is born

Chilling image from the History of Trucking Museum

ANOTHER VICTIM OF ADVERTISING

ACTUAL HUMAN CANNONBALL

33

EARLY HOMOSAPIENS LAUGHING AT ROCKS SHAPED LIKE A COMPUTER

HELLO, EARTHLING! WE ARE BENEVOLENT BEINGS FROM ANOTHER PLANET, IDENTICAL TO YOU IN EVERY WAY — EXCEPT THAT OUR APPENDIX HAS A *PURPOSE!*

41

Day 752 — My captors continue to taunt me with bizarre little dangling objects. They dine lavishly on fresh meat, while I am forced to eat dry cereal. The only thing that keeps me going is the hope of escape, and the mild satisfaction I get from ruining the occasional piece of furniture. Tomorrow I may eat another houseplant.

FINDING THE CAT'S DIARY

PIRARO.

...IF JILL ST. JOHN WERE MADE A SAINT *AND* HAD A STREET NAMED AFTER HER.

St. Jill St. John St.

SIGN COMPANY HUMOR

PIRARO

49

HEE HEE HEE HEE HOO HEE HA HA HEE HEE HEE
HOO HOO HEE HEE
HEE HOO HOO HEH HEH HOO HAHA

AMONG THE FIRST SPECIES TO DISAPPEAR AT THE HANDS OF MAN WAS THE COUSIN OF THE HOWLER MONKEY, THE SNICKERING MONKEY.

PIRARO.

THE RATINGS PLUMMET WHEN WE FEATURE IN-DEPTH ANALYSIS, SO INSTEAD, LET'S FIND OUT WHAT *SQUEAKY, THE TALKING CHIHUAHUA* THINKS OF THE JOB THE PRESIDENT HAS BEEN DOING...

PIRARO.

63

AT THE MALL WITH NEIL ARMSTRONG

THE BATTLE BETWEEN CABLE TV AND THE NETWORKS

NEVER COMFORTABLE WITH THE HEADHUNTER SOCIETY IN WHICH HE WAS RAISED, KOTAMAUI EVENTUALLY MOVED TO CALIFORNIA AND OPENED A WIG SHOP.

PIRARO.

INTERNATIONAL SIGNAGE SCHOOL OF ART

PIRARO.

SHAME OF THE SLEEPWALKER

PARAKEETS PETEY & TWEETS MAKE PLANS TO FORM A "GANGAKEETS."

73

TRAGEDY STRUCK AN OAK CLIFF LETTER CARRIER AND HIS WIFE, A REAL ESTATE AGENT, WHEN THEY INADVERTENTLY SWAPPED HIS CAN OF MACE WITH HER CAN OF BREATH FRESHENER... BOTH WERE RUSHED TO CITY HOSPITAL AROUND MIDDAY.

PIRARO.

BY ORDER OF THE CAPTAIN, "PEG-LEG BILL" WILL NOW BE CALLED "TAP DANCE-CHALLENGED BILL"...."ONE-EYED JAKE" IS NOW "WINK-INHIBITED JAKE"....CAPTAIN HOOK HIMSELF WILL BE CALLED "THE NON-JUGGLING CAPTAIN." AND THE REST OF YOU SCURVY KNAVES WILL BE REFERRED TO AS THE "VITAMIN C DISADVANTAGED."

PIRATES GONE P.C.

PIRARO.

SPOTTING THE
LOCH NESS MOBSTER

78

OFTEN MISTAKEN FOR HIS DREADED COUSIN, THE GRIM REAPER, THE GRIM GOLFER NEVER HAS TO WAIT IN LINE TO TEE OFF.

I'M ON MY WAY TO THE PRESS CONFERENCE TO ANSWER THE PATERNITY ALLEGATIONS AGAINST YOU BY THE COCKER SPANIEL IN IOWA. HOW DO YOU WANT ME TO HANDLE IT? — SHALL I BARK OR WHINE?

WHAT IT WILL BE LIKE AFTER THE COUNTRY HAS GONE TO THE DOGS

INVENTION OF THE BARROW—
FOUR YEARS BEFORE THE
INVENTION OF THE WHEEL

THE EARLY DAYS OF CARTOON MEDICINE

SLUG POSSE

93

INSTITUTION FOR THE CRIMINALLY INANE

TEEN-AGE TARZAN

INSIDE THE STATUE OF LIBERTY

109

The CREATIVE PROCESS
an Autobiographical Documentary